Passive Income

3 Proven Business Models That Generate Online Revenue to Achieve Financial Freedom

Table of contents

Passive income by Scot Harvey

Introduction

I want to thank you and congratulate you for downloading the book, "*Social Anxiety: Guide to Overcome Shyness, Shame, Social Phobia and to Understand How to Help Yourself to Achieve Social Freedom* ".

This book contains proven steps and strategies on how to realize the life that you desire the most, and have the social freedom that you want and you always dreamed to have.

You have in front of you a book that offers you a change.

Perhaps you've thinking or you were told that you suffer from social anxiety disorder or social phobia. This would help you understand that you have the restraint or fear of contact with other people, contacts that you find threatening for prestige or your reputation, fear of being judged or misrepresented, fear of being taken for what In fact you're not. So better try to avoid this situation, behavior that led you mostly to loneliness.

In this book I suggest you make a change. This change is based on my firm belief that the so-called "social anxiety disorder" or "social phobia" mental illness is not real, but only a "medicalization" of accentuated traits of psychic structure of people. It is the fact that shyness, embarrassment and shame that some people felt sharply in social relationships, was taken as pathological as being the expression of a mental disorder that exhibits the specific medical diagnosis and treatment. The "medicalization" of human behavior makes people seek external help and to forget its own resources to manage this situation.

I do not believe in this approach. Furthermore, I believe that this approach is harmful to an individual with such issues will be considered sick, which it will lead to greater isolation from others with the belief that everyone around you will see in this light and so it feels carries a stigma.

My belief is that the so-called social anxiety disorder or social phobia is nothing but an exaggeration of normal human emotions, such as shyness, embarrassment and shame, emotions which in different proportions to have any man. The fact that some of us are more sensitive to these emotions empowers the Court did not anyone consider them sick.

4

I suggest you change the interpretation they give your problems with these emotions and consider them as part of its own way of social interaction. I'll introduce a suite of techniques that you can manage these emotions so that they do not affect your position in social space. For the track i must tell you from the beginning that I will use the term social anxiety as a broad concept that gathers in it different aspects of an individual who shows varying degrees of exaggeration of shyness, embarrassment and shame when they meet others and different origin and ways of interpreting their significance. In any case, the social anxiety used in this book does not mean a disease but a trait or condition of our mental life. Interpreted in this way, shyness, embarrassment and shame can be interpreted so that you may believe that you are able to modify them so that they no longer interfere with the way you behave in social situations.

So you will understand that you are at the root of these problems are and the origin of their change for the better. This is the ultimate goal of this book to get you to help yourself in case of shyness, embarrassment and shame accentuated.

Thanks again for downloading this book, I hope you enjoy it!

Chapter 1

What is passive income?

Passive income 101

Passive income is that type of income that you can create to receive on regular basis with no effort to maintain it or very little effort. The primarily focus is on creating the income source that is going going to generate the passive income for you. We are going to concentrate on passive income generated online even though are very popular passive income streams outside of "internet world" such as :

- Any type of property income that you have
- The earnings that you get from a business which you are involved as investor , owner or merchant
- Rent from having a property rented
- Receiving interest from a bank account that you own
- Royalties being paid for intellectual properties such as art, film, music
- Any many many other

I want to begin this book by clarifying the concept of passive income.
I prefer to define passive income as the kind of income that continues to enter our accounts even after I stopped working. Another name for passive income would be residual income.
By contrast, active income is the type of income you get only so long as we continue to work. If you receive a salary and give you resign or are fired, most likely you will not be paid. Maybe you can get some compensation or redundancy payments, but one thing is clear: the boss will not continue to pay your salary while you see every day at work.
Similarly, if you are self employed and have their own customers, they will pay only as long as you work for them. This is also an active form of income. As an independent contractor you will have a
a more flexible schedule, but you still have to work continuously to earn money.

If you exchange a source of passive income, you will continue to earn money from it no matter if you work for it or decide to retire. It is possible to deposit a serious effort to put the wheels in motion, but eventually you reach the point where the source of passive income becomes functional. From that moment you cease to work because the money will continue to enter the account regardless of the efforts.

Passive income does not mean getting a single payment, such as the sale of a building or a stake. Passive income is income source characterized by continuity in time.

However, passive income is not the same with permanent income. Some sources can bring passive income for several years, while others may continue producing for decades or even centuries, over several generations. However, for one reason or another, all sources of passive income will be exhausted at some point.

It should also know that passive income is income not 100% sure. As Helen Keller wrote, "Security is mostly a superstition hand."

Also, not all sources of passive income is 100% passive. Most sources of income requires a minimum of maintenance activity. Sometimes this activity is very simple and only involves checking e-mails. Sometimes it takes something more than that.

Passive income in my opinion its one of the greatest income types that you can develop and for sure I consider it something that everybody should learn more about it and try it.

Nowadays with the internet and the technological revolution that we are being part of the global economy its in constant changing and so are the ways we earn our living. Please from anywhere from the globe with almost no experience in the field that are getting into can make more money using the internet then an expert with 20+ years experience working as an employee and will less and less effort. Processes are being automated more and more people are getting in because its pretty simple and it doesn't require:

- to money money to start a business, nowadays you can start a business with less than 1000$ or with less than 100$, giving a spoiler about what we are going to discuss (selling e-books online, having your own website/blog, making affiliate marketing, selling your own physical product)
- creating passive income online doesn't require to be in fixed place, you can work from anywhere over the globe as long as you have a computer and an internet connection
- the possibility to automate all the processes in the business by hiring virtual assistants and have cheap employees paid by hour delivering the exact result that you want and not worrying for the fact that you are going to pay and employees not working at full potential, working on project the person that you employee its going to be more interested to get work done and get their money, a very important thing in my opinion to optimize your costs in your business
- the fact that you can work less than 4 hours per week as in Tim Ferris book "4 hour work-week" or even less then 4 hours per month, the advantage processes in your business, another reason why passive income online its such a good thing.

This is not a get rich quick scheme!

I want to be clear, creating passive income online its not a get rich quick scheme, it requires effort, can be hard, ca be easy, but it is not a get rich quick scheme! It will require to invest time, energy, stress, TO MAINTAIN it won't require a lot of time and energy ! Depending on the business model that you decide your to go with you will may have also a short learning curve and quick profit usually by selling informational products like e-books or a long learning curve and more bigger profits by going for example with creating a brand, a website that can sustain your business, basically being the platform for your business. If you decide to go with kindle publishing, Amazon FBA, Affiliate marketing, online Courses, niche sites and many many others. Keep reading with get more in depth with more relevant business models that create passive income for you, what will require and how you can get started as soon as possible.

Chapter 2

How to make money with kindle publishing

When you are saying online publishing and selling e-books online you are talking about one of the most frequent approached business models with fast results and big profits, nowadays selling e-books its very easy to do, you don't really need to have your own website ranked in google, to spend time to write the content of your books and spend money doing all the marketing and also investing in advertising.

Getting started with kindle publishing

KDP or Kindle direct publishing it's the platform offered by Amazon for publishers to produce e-books to publish them and create really fast passive income. Amazon it's the platform that you use to publish your book, you don't have to worry about traffic, amazon it's the biggest online marketplace so traffic its going to be assured by them, they do all the marketing you need, you won't have to invest in advertising, they have the platform for you to upload your book, so you won't have to worry about creating a website and they have the clients you need to serve them the products that they want. Let me break down the process for you:

Registration

You will have to go to amazon.com and register for a kindle publishing account, that would take you a couple of minutes, after that you should have access to you Kdp account and should be ready to start publishing books. Below I've attached a figure with registration form and how should look like.

Finding profitable niches to publish books

Now that you have you account set up its time to search for profitable niches to publish books. The process its pretty simple but a lot of people get it done wrong, it represents over 70% of your business success so I advice you to be very careful in this process.

Amazon its helps us so much that it even shows us what is selling, they offer information about what is hot right now and what its not selling. So without any details go to amazon.com and then to department section where you will be looking for "kindle store". Kindle Store it's the place where we are going to publish our books where clients will find two types of books non-fiction, those that are treating any kind of subjects in amazon's categories and non-fiction, romance drama and any type of story.

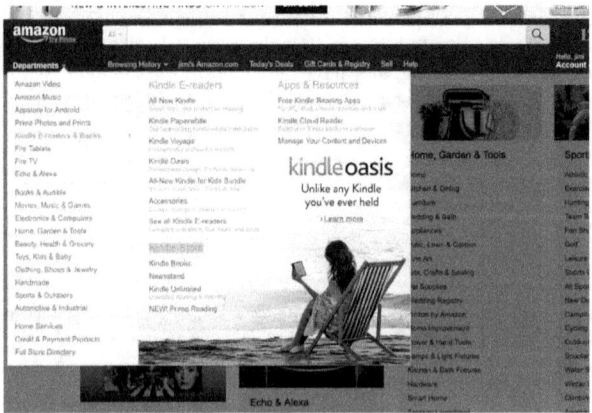

We are going to take the most amount of time on niche research because it's the most important thing in your business. If you are deciding to publish a book in a niche that its no audience and its no demand the obvious result will be that you are not going to make any money there and also the if you are going to publish a book in a niche that its to crowded you will now be able to rank your book and make any sales.

So that being said are a couple of criteria's that a book has to met to be making a good amount of money per month:

- The Best seller rank(BSR) must be under 100.000, preferably as low as possible indicates there are money to be made in that niche, over 100.000 rank won't make sell so good.

Product Details

File Size: 291 KB
Print Length: 22 pages
Simultaneous Device Usage: Unlimited
Publication Date: August 30, 2016
Sold by: Amazon Digital Services LLC
Language: English
ASIN: B01LA6P7BY
Text-to-Speech: Enabled
X-Ray: Not Enabled
Word Wise: Enabled
Lending: Not Enabled
Enhanced Typesetting: Enabled
Amazon Best Sellers Rank: #633,028 Paid in Kindle Store (See Top 100 Paid in Kindle Store)
   #1235 in Kindle Store > Kindle Short Reads > 45 minutes (22-32 pages) > Self-Help
   #1299 in Kindle Store > Kindle Short Reads > 45 minutes (22-32 pages) > Business & Money
   #1850 in Kindle Store > Kindle eBooks > Nonfiction > Self-Help > Happiness

Would you like to tell us about a lower price?
If you are a seller for this product, would you like to suggest updates to the product page?

- The number of reviews that are in that market, you must have in attention that the more reviews the books have the harder will be to rank you book on first page among other books, everything under 100 reviews will be pretty realizable.

- The market that you enter must have over 1500 results, everything its less than 1500 results will show that the niche its too small, if are a lot for books over 1500, lets say for example 10.000 results the niche its too crowded.

- The book must have at least 2 months tenure on amazon, the newer it's the niche the more instable will be, because of the boost that amazon gives to your book when its new released

The process of creating an e-book

Having your book done couldn't be more simple then now, you can hire a ghostwriter for that task and are a lot of options available out there. I strongly recommend going on a website like upwork.com and post a "Job" asking for writers, usually the rates are for about 1$ per 100 words written.

How long should be your book? Having a book written in non-fiction usually you can go with between 5000 words and 10000 words that would be a good length for your book. Customers are not looking for a long book they want concise information to consume it and to gain a lot of value from it so a short book book would serve them more, usually I recommend around 8000 words.

Usually it take up to 7 days to have the book done, enough time to get done the next thing that you need, cover!

The process of creating an e-book cover

Outsourcing it's awesome, you can have somebody hired to do your book and in that time you can hire somebody to create your cover. For that task you can get a great graphic designer on fiverr.com and have it done for 5$ or even 2,5$ depending on the rates of the designer you are working with. The delivery time for that usually its about 1 to 2 days.

Publish your book on amazon!

After getting your book and you cover done all you have to do its to go on amazon and publish your book, a very simple process!

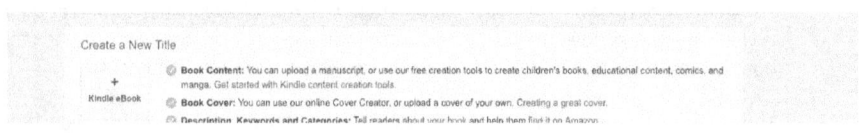

The process its pretty simple and nice to follow, now you have to complete the fields with your e-book title that should include your keyword from the niche that you selected and the subtitle of that. Upload your e-book document on amazon and the cover of your book and then choose the keywords that you want your book to have and the categories for your book, you can choose up to two categories for your book and you are done! Now set the price of your book, I advice you to keep it around 2.99$ and now you can publish it on amazon!

Market your book!

Marketing its very important to make your book to sale, now that you have your book available on amazon all you have to do its to promote it, you can submit your book to sites that are promoting e-books and also on Facebook groups that promoting e-books. Getting reviews also can be done by hiring a Virtual assistant on Facebook groups! If you want to find out more about how to market your book I strongly advice to search for courses on "kindle publishing" or even better hire a coach that can make advice you and make the learning curve even smaller giving you all the insights that you need!

Hope you will enjoy this business model and create your first passive income stream online!

Chapter 3

How to make money selling physical products(Amazon FBA)

What are the origins how Amazon?

Amazon is an American company of e-commerce selling physical products informational products and also could computing services. The company has been founded in July 5, 1994 and the founder of the company its Jeff Bezos. Its one of the largest internet based retailers you can find anything you need to buy like DVD-s, CD-s, music, movies, books, furniture, games, tables, phones and many other products. In 2015 the total assets of the company were about US $65.444 billion. The code of the site its written in extension with C++ and Java.

As the story sais everything started in the backyard of Jeff Bezos and slowly started to extend, since Amazon Kindle devices debuted on market amazon sold millions and millions of electronic books one of the main products of Amazon and a big part of their business. When you are thinking about Amazon you are thinking to a gigantic website like Google, like Facebook, like Instagram.

As time went by people grown trust and the level of satisfaction that amazon assured to customers encouraged them to sell their own physical products.

Selling your own physical products requires:

- To be dedicated to what are you doing and to have a passion to the product that you are selling on market, to take it serious and realize that you are building a business
- To invest as much time as needed in the early phase to create the product and to place it on market
- To invest money upfront you can invest little as 500$ or even 5000$ to start your Amazon business.
- Develop your strategy and how you are going to promote your product out there and satisfy your clients
- Think on long term, think about your clients needs and how important it is to acquire a client
- Creating an e-mail list, collecting e-mails from customers, creating a relationship with them, treat them with respect and they also are going to treat you with respect.

You are not just a "Seller" as you may think, you are building a long term sustainable business, once the effort has been but all you have now to do its to enjoy the results. Creating your platform outside Amazon will strengthen your business and start competing with big brands in your niche out there.

What is Amazon FBA ?

What is Amazon FBA or Fulfillment by Amazon and the best way to describe it will be as a service offered by Amazon for giving you the opportunity to sell physical products on Amazon's platform. After having your own physical product listed Amazon will handle customer support and all processes to have the product delivered to you customer. They will handle the order, they will ship the product they will handle the returns and any customer needs. Basically Amazon its getting a lot of work done for you, all you have to take care of it's to have a good product and correctly market it.

To get started with Amazon FBA you will have to :
- Register for a seller account
- Create a listing for your product
- Create your own product to sell
- Ship the inventory to amazon
- Promote it on internet and get sales!

One of the biggest advantages with Amazon FBA its that after having all the systems in place you can work less then four hours per week and with your own team you will not worry anymore about business.

How much money can I make on Amazon FBA selling my own product?

The amount of money that you will be making depends totally on you, the product that you choose to sell, the production costs that you have for your product, how much money you invest in adverting, what is the price that you are selling your product for, how much competition its in your niche and so on. Having an estimation you can make 4 figure per month profit, 5 figure per month profit or as I saw in some cases even 7-8 figures per year profit.

Lets get into the process of selling your product on Amazon

Before creating your own physical product and having hundreds of dollars invested you should check if there is a market for your product so that means to make a market research like we did for kindle publishing business. That's a crucial step because as we discussed at the beginning of the book if it's not a market for your product you won't make any sales there and if the market its too crowded you won't be able to enter on that market and rank for your product so pay big attention to this step when you are conducting your research!

#1 Market research

Amazon best seller list its what we are going to look for because its one of the most safe fast and reliable tool that we can use to see what is selling and what its not selling right now now. ITS VERY important to look for relevant keywords in the market that you want to get in and to have your product identified by that

#2 Search criteria

When you will be searching for your product you must have in mind a couple of criteria's:

- Try to find small products, light products that are easy to ship so in this way you will avoid having big shipping costs and will be easy to ship for your client and usually small and light products are not breakable, avoid products that have glass in them.
- Look for products that can assure you a profit margin from 30 to 60% after paying your taxes, manufacture costs, advertising costs and so on.
- Try as much as possible to avoid electrical products, products that are breakable or may need special conditions to transport.
- Look for the price of the product now to be to small because will be hard to have a good return but also not to big because will pretty expensive to produce stock for your product, you don't want to invest thousands of dollars without knowing if your product its going to sell or not.

#3 Take a look on the category under the products

When searching for products please keep in mind the best seller rank of the product to be at least 5000 or lower and should be priced between 25$ and 100$, that would be a reasonable selling price and will give you the possibility to get good profit margins. Keep in mind the weight of your product not the dimensions of your product, it would be great you product to weight from 0,1 pounds to 2 pounds, keep in mind that the smaller the dimensions and the weight the better for shipping.

FIND A SUPPLIER FOR YOUR PRODUCT

Now that you identified the product that you want to sell its time to find a supplier and start working on your product. Private labelling its best thing for customizing the items or items that you want to sell on Amazon.

The best place I can recommend you to go its alibaba.com its one of the biggest marketplaces where you can find supplier which are selling while label products.

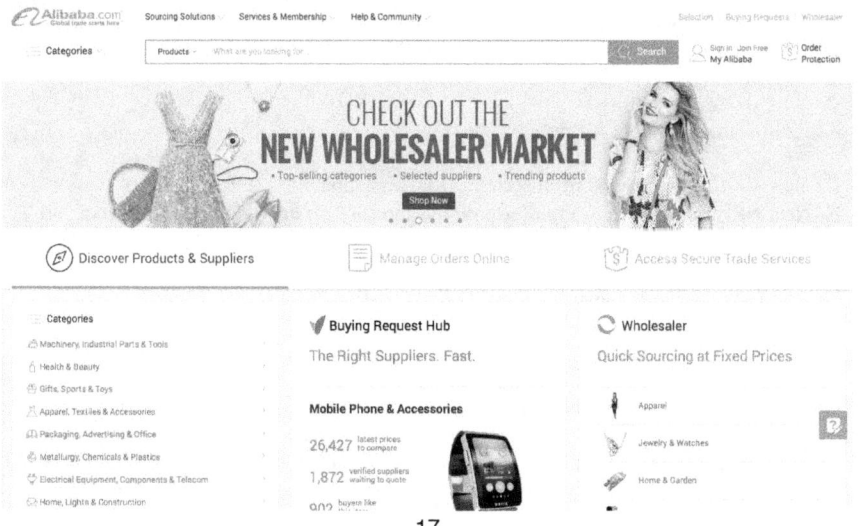

After registering for an account on alibaba.com just search for your product and start compering prices, quality and what your supplier can offer. Prepare a set of questions for your supplier like:

- the price per unit
- the minimum amount that you can order
- how much can you customize your product
- how safe it's the business relationship with the supplier

The process can be pretty slow but its very important to pay attention to the process, to get every step done right, consolidating the relationship with your supplier it's a very important step and also to get sure that your product its high quality, your customers won't forgive and mistake in the manufacture process, you have to deliver de best quality possible.

Time to get barcodes for your product! You can get with 10$ barcodes for your product, every unit must have a code applied, after purchasing barcodes you can send them to your supplier and he can attach that to your product before shipping it!

Get design done!

When you are customizing your product you may need logos, graphics and so on to be done. You can go on fiverr.com and have it done in a short period of time and very inexpensive.

Set up your product listing

This is another crucial step in this business model. If you want your product to be sold on Amazon you must pay big attention to your listing because represents the way your product is being displayed on Amazon, how your customers will see it and how they are going to judge it they are going to buy it or not!

Steps to follow to create your listing!

1. Sign in into your seller central account from amazon.com
2. Next click on "seller account information" and click on Upgrade to upgrade to a "Pro Merchant" account, a paid account that will allow you to sell unlimited units and you will not be limited on the number of units that you can sell.
3. Go to Manage your inventory and click on "Create a Product detail page"
4. Create categories for your product, categorize it.

Very important to have in attention !

1. The name of your product : The name of your product it is very important because will include keywords after your customer will search for your product and will influence your

rank on amazon. It must include in the first words the most important keywords that you want to rank for and then rest of the benefits directly in title. The idea its not to look good but to be efficient ranking on amazon.

2. The brand name : I strongly advice you to try to create brand on amazon, in this way your customers will find easily your products and also will help ranking, keep in mind the competition its big you must difference yourself in any way you can.

3. The product description: the product description its very important because will help for:
- Better rankings, in description basically you are including keywords to rank, its part of Amazon SEO, also this is representing an opportunity to learn SEO, another good skill to have
- Including benefits of your product, making an aesthetic page that would attract customers to buy
- Relationship with the person that wants to purchase your product, it will difference your customers and people that you want to be part of your business

4. Pricing : Pricing its very important to difference yourself on market, usually it's a price that all your competitors use with small differences, I advice you to study their strategy on pricing and not to go with your price too low because in client perception will look like a cheap product that won't inspire quality, don't be afraid to put a price that higher!
5. Photos: Hire a photograph, don't be cheap, your product will be judged as valuable or not by photos, be sure to hire a good photograph to get high quality pictures of your product and look as good as possible, you want to create an experience of how would be to use your product and how great they are going to feel to have it just by looking at photos.

Get reviews to your product

As use talked in the first part of the book, reviews play a big role in creating trust on market, your client wants to be sure that makes the best choice when its buying a product, he must like your product, like your company and like yourself.
This relationship mostly can be realized through reviews, a advice you to get a couple more reviews than your competition to consolidate your position as a trustful brand and make anybody interested in your listing.
Social proof, anything that reviews are representing its social proof, be sure to get reviews but also the quality of your reviews counts a lot! Be sure to have detailed reviews describing the benefits of your product, advantages and so on, would be nice to have pictures in reviews with your product being used by the person that its reviewing the product.

How to get reviews?

The reviews process its very simple to be done and can be done using more methods:
- Send a couple of units to your friends and family to test the product and ask for a sincere opinion about the quality of your product and how can be improved for a better experience. Don't forget to review your product on Amazon
- Tomoson.com it's a website where you can list your product to give away to people to review it, they are going to receive your product using a promo code and in exchange they are going to review it and post the review also on their blog, Facebook, Instagram or any

other platform you prefer. You can even ask them to make a video and post it on YouTube, Tomoson.com represents a very good way to drive traffic on your listing and this approach can help you when launching your product get best seller rank pumped and also the giveaway will be a good method to help you rank your product. Keep in mind though, if your product doesn't deliver a good experience and it's not good quality you won't receive a good review from the person that you sent the product.

- You can post your product on a Facebook group with other amazon seller that are looking to get reviews for their product and you can exchange products and also to review other people's product to get an idea of what is coming on amazon but also to get a more ample idea of how others perceive your product

- You can post your product on a Facebook group with people that are consuming the product that you are selling and in my opinion this is the best way to get reviews, from actual people that would really buy your product and would need it. Sending promo codes so they can get the product and also make a comparison with other products. For example you are selling a yoga mat you can post that you give away 10, 20 yoga mat for people that do you yoga to test that and offer a sincere opinion, you can give away as many units as you consider you need, I recommend your giveaway to be correlated with the level of competition on market, the bigger the competition the more units I recommend to give away for review.

I totally recommend to get reviews also because in this process you are getting your best seller rank up and up and that would help you to keep your product on first page and in their attention. I strongly recommend to get more information's about the business model that you want to get in, a strong documentation about your product but also about the customer that you are serving, its very important to understand!

Chapter 4

How to make money with affiliate marketing

Affiliate marketing

Affiliate marketing it's a great way to produce income nowadays, the best part is that can be integrated in a lot of business models that you are doing, the most important thing its having a big fallowing and marketing as good as possible to your fallowing.

So what is affiliate marketing?

Affiliate marketing as I said in the first paragraph It's an income stream that can be generated even if you are a publisher or retail store. Affiliate marketing can be done using a promotion or just by posting affiliate links inside your platform, website, Facebook page, Instagram page, twitter page or any other channel that you have a lot of people following you. People click the link that you put on and they if they make a sale you are receiving a commission. Its that simple to make affiliate marketing basically all you need it's a big following and an affiliate program that you are part of. The most know affiliate programs that you can join are Amazon Affiliates, an affiliate program offered by amazon where you can promote products from amazon and another one being Clickbank.com where you can promote any type of product you would like (fitness programs, money making programs and so on).

Advertisers often like to make affiliate marketing to promote their own products, adding their own physical products or informational programs to this type of websites. The biggest advantage it's the fact that you don't have to worry about creating the product, about customer support, about shipping the product, in case it's a physical product, improving it any other concern related to the product itself.

We are going to get more deeper into affiliate marketing that its made on blogs or niche sites, a business model that became very popular and generating good profits and gives you the possibility to live a 4 hour work week like in Tim Ferris book.

Niche Websites

Keyword Research

When it come to online business keyword research its one of the most important things that we have to take care of. Keyword research may represent more than 70% of your success either you are doing kindle publishing, Amazon FBA or Niche Websites. Keyword research its made on Google's search engine. Due to the fact that this is the most popular search engine used we are going to take in consideration the most the results that we get on Google. Its important at the end of our keyword research we are finding a niche not to crowded but also not to small, here the way we do search engine optimization it's a little different than on amazon, we are ranking not for a product but for the hole website. When ranking website on google its very important to be very careful with SEO technique used:
- White hat SEO – being the right way to do SEO
- Grey hat SEO - being a little risky
- Black hat SEO – risking to have your website down by Google

When conducting the research I recommend you to try a website like Jaxxy.com, a keyword research platform, after getting some niches ideas you can test then and get some data to analyze to see how if we found a niche to go into or not. You can try the trial version offered by Jaaxy.com to get used with keyword research.

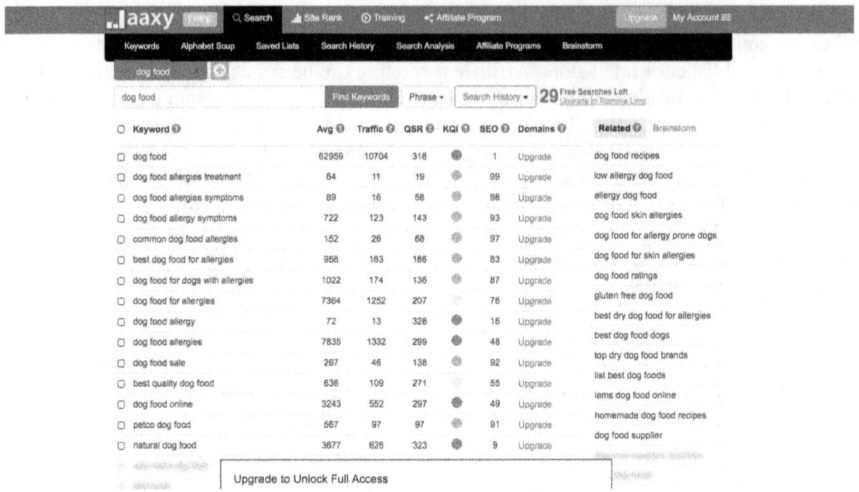

In the image above you can see a trial account made for the purpose of this example. I've already made a search on "dog food" to see what kind of results we can get so :
- The " Avg " column representing the number of results that we get for the search and the phrases that we can use, usually its better to the average over 5000 searches per month
- "Traffic" column representing visits to your website if you get on first page for that keyword ranking.
- "QSR" column usually its better to be as low as possible preferably under 100, keywords that are under 100 I recommend to be used
- "KQI" column the best its when its green indicates that we found good keywords
- "SEO" I suggest to be as high as possible, as close it can be to 100

Domain Research

Domain research its what we are interested after getting an idea on what niche we are going to create a website after we find keywords in the parameters that we are interested in.

For buying domains I suggest godaddy.com very simple to use. I strongly suggest you to look for .com domains . I suggest to check for domain availability not just .com but also on .net or your own country. Below I've attached a print screen with the results on godday.com

22

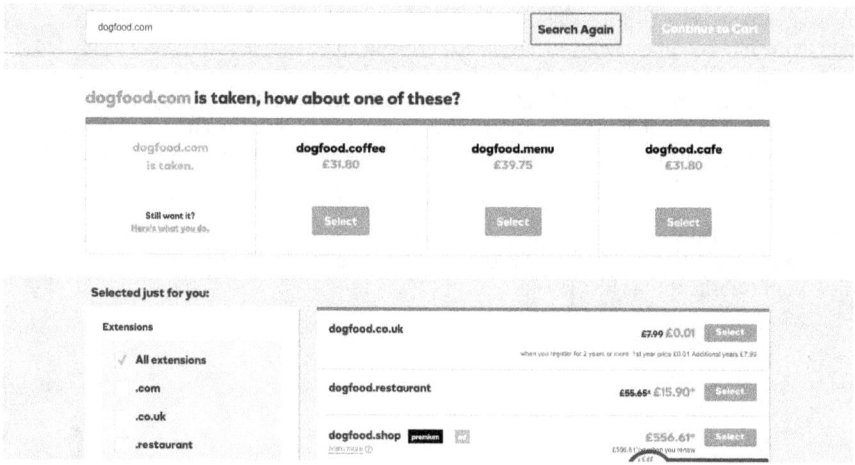

WordPress Theme

After purchasing domain and hosting for your website, you can install your WordPress Theme. I suggest you to use WordPress for the fact that it's very easy user and to customize. You can buy a WordPress for 50$ or even 20$ or if you don't have money to invest it's no problem there are a lot of great free WordPress themes out there that you can try out. It's a very simple process that should take you around 15-30 minutes to complete, if you feeling like needing some help I advice you to consult YouTube, are plenty of videos out there that take you step by step to complete this process.

Website Structure & Content Planning

Now that you have your website ready you are good to go. Don't be a perfectionist, things just have to look good and work good on your website, people will be visiting your website for your content and information's that you share , adding logos, banners, advertising its something that can be done easily after you start developing an audience.

Website Structure I recommend you to keep it simple at first a simple header with a contact page, about me page and recommended recourses. A simple header and a simple footer will work just fine as long as the text it's being framed good in page and also every article has good pictures.

Content Planning its very important you can't just publish content without having a structure in mind before of how every article should look like and also how articles are going to lay the "story" that you are telling to the reader. Either you are doing a niche site or authority site its important to have a clear image of what you what to communicate to the person that its reading you website.

Affiliate links

And the most important part, affiliate links to products, this is the source of your income. Its very important through every article that you post to add affiliate links. People will be very pleased to see good content, useful content that is bringing value but also to see the link that they can click on and made a purchase, don't be afraid of putting as many affiliate links as possible, people often feel uncomfortable to add affiliate links, customers will appreciate its pretty uncomfortable after you get some good information and want to make purchase to go again on google and make a search, give to the customer what he needs.

I recommend you to write articles over 1000 words for better rankings also to keep in mind that you always can outsource this task to a ghost writer. Do a strong documentation on SEO and how to better rank your website for the best results.

Conclusion

Thank you again for downloading this book!

I hope this book was able to help you to understand and overcome social anxiety.

The next step is to be sure that you fully understand the information, also apply it and read it as frequently as necessary.

Finally, if you enjoyed this book, then I'd like to ask you for a favor, would you be kind enough to leave a review for this book on Amazon? It'd be greatly appreciated!

If you enjoyed the FIRST BOOK and want to be updated when the next book appears on Social Anxiety click on the following link :

http://eepurl.com/cbUZ45

_____

Thank you and good luck!